MAXIMIZE YOUR MARRIAGE

B. Courtney McBath

CREATION
HOUSE PRESS

Maximize Your Marriage
by B. Courtney McBath
Published by Creation House Press
A part of Strang Communications Company
600 Rinehart Road
Lake Mary, Florida 32746
www.creationhouse.com

All Scripture quotations are from the New American Standard Bible. Copyright © 1960, 1962, 1963, 1968, 1971, 1972, 1973, 1975, 1977 by the Lockman Foundation. Used by permission. (www.Lockman.org)

Cover design by Karen Gonzalves

Library of Congress Catalog Card Number: 2002100149
International Standard Book Number: 0-88419-885-5

02 03 04 05 8765432
Printed in the United States of America

For my wife

Acknowledgments

I would like to honor my lovely wife of more than twenty years, Janeen, to whom this book is dedicated. Through you I have learned so many lessons about life and love—hopefully, I've managed to capture some of them in this book.

I also must thank our pastor and copastor, the Reverends Richard and Theresa Hilton, for years of love and support. Special thanks to our pastors who gave us our premarital counsel, Bishop and Mrs. Gilbert A. Thompson, Sr.

My staff worked tirelessly to help me complete this book. I especially would like to thank Patrick Walker, my business manager; Patrice Perry, my business development consultant; Candace McCrary, my assistant editor; and Stacy Mattingly, my editor-in-chief.

Table of Contents

Foreword

Male and female. Boy and girl. Son and daughter. Man and woman. Groom and bride. Husband and wife. However you label the sexes, one fact remains: We are different. And differences are just the beginning of our problems and joys in marriage.

Many couples enter marriage without proper marital training, and they wind up bewildered when trouble comes. Unrealistic—sometimes "storybook"—expectations only increase the strain. When you consider the additional challenges of a dysfunctional childhood home or a lack of maturity in either spouse, you can understand why so few marriages, even Christian marriages, survive in America today. Marriage's precarious condition makes this book especially timely and essential.

I have served Courtney and Janeen McBath as pastor and friend for nearly two decades, and they are just like you and me. They are perfectly human. Their marriage has succeeded not because they've had it easy. As a matter of fact, with five children and a large ministry to oversee, the McBaths may face more obstacles than most families. Instead, what has fortified their relationship is their faithful application of biblical principles. As the Scripture teaches, "By wisdom a house is built, and by understanding it is established" (Prov. 24:3).

You too can access the power of God's principles and cultivate your marriage. Absorb the teaching in these pages. Apply the wisdom related here to your relationship. Let the Word of God work in your life. If you do these things consistently, then in time your marriage will become more resilient and your family more secure.

RICHARD HILTON, SENIOR FOUNDING PASTOR
CALVARY CHURCH
JOHNSON CITY, TENNESSEE
DECEMBER 2001

Introduction

I trace the inception of this book back to February 1999—in particular, to an evening when I was preparing to teach our Wednesday night service. At that time, I was teaching on the issues of relationship development and the marriage covenant. I began my work for this specific message by brainstorming: What practical steps could help spouses build successful marriages? I jotted down some Bible-based habits that had proved invaluable in my own marriage. When I finished, there were more than a dozen steps.

As I taught about the steps that Wednesday night, I sensed an unusually strong measure of the Holy Spirit's presence in our midst. The tape sales from the service set records, and the volume of incoming calls following the service's television broadcast astonished everyone. One of our ministers reported that men at the shipyard where he worked were trying to get copies of the tape without even having heard the message. Married folks at the church began to post the steps on their refrigerators; single folks began to memorize the steps. I was overwhelmed. At that point, I knew a book was needed. What you have in hand is the result of my efforts.

Readers who are not Christians can apply at least

seven of the twelve steps addressed in this book. The principles will work regardless of your religious beliefs, as long as you genuinely love your spouse and commit to giving your best in the marriage. Consider the second step: *Remove the word* divorce *from your vocabulary.* Anyone can do this. You and your spouse can decide to live it out, tough it out and love it out until you are separated by death. Keep your promise, maintain your commitment and enjoy the benefits!

To implement the final five steps, you need to have made a meaningful commitment to Jesus Christ and His Word. Marriage is a God-given institution; to enjoy it to the fullest you need God's participation. For readers who require understanding in this area, I have included a clear, concise, but nonconfrontational explanation of Christian commitment just before chapter eight.

As you learn to practice the principles outlined here, those of you who are Christians may find that the Lord leads you to married people who are struggling in Christ-less marriages and need encouragement. Let these steps to marital success open a door for you to share the love of Jesus with those who are hurting.

Finally, let me give you some instruction on how to read this book:

- Read it like a textbook, taking notes and reviewing concepts you don't understand. Pay close attention to the list of reference books at the end of chapter six and use these books as resources.

- Read it like a how-to book. Apply the truths

in each chapter *as you read*. Don't wait until you finish the book—that will be too late! Write out a personal plan for implementing the steps in your own marriage. If you're engaged, then make sure your fiancé or fiancée reads along with you.

- Read it like a maintenance manual you might purchase to help you work on a car or computer. Treat your marriage like a well-designed machine that needs regular care. I'm sure you'll agree that when it comes to fine-tuning your marriage, you don't want someone else doing the job!

- Read it like a novel that takes you to destinations you've not yet visited. Let your vision for your marriage expand as you process the Word of God. Let your faith increase for higher levels of fulfillment in marriage.

After more than twenty years of applying these truths in relationship with my wife, Janeen, I can assure you the benefits are manifold.

Receive everything in this book as if it were for you—because it is!

CHAPTER 1

Make It Your Business to Please One Another

⌇

Establish a Common Goal

Marriage has little to do with getting your own needs met and everything to do with meeting the needs of someone else.

Someone needs to tell single people not to get married until they're ready to die. Few married couples begin their journey knowing the truth. They walk into marriage blind and end up confounded when the time comes to start sacrificing. The truth is, marriage has little to do with getting your own needs met and everything to do with meeting the needs of someone else.

When you move from single life into marriage, your God-given purpose changes. The apostle Paul explains the difference in his first letter to the Corinthians.

"One who is unmarried is concerned about the things of the Lord, how he may please the Lord; but one who is married is concerned about the things of the world, how he may please his wife" (1 Cor. 7:32–33). Paul relates this to us almost matter-of-factly, as if our calling in marriage were obvious. We need it to be obvious. If no one told you before you got married, allow me: You now live to please your spouse.

Once you understand your purpose as a married man or woman, make it your priority. Bringing satisfaction to your spouse should be your business, your livelihood. We go to work sick, tired, mad and often broke. But because our work is our business, we tough it out. Many people quit on their marriages when they become sick and tired. They quit because they haven't made pleasing one another their business. It's only something they do when they feel up to it. Be forewarned—until you put pleasing your spouse at the center of your marriage, frustration and chaos will plague your relationship.

God's Word tells us a man should leave his father and mother, cling to his wife and become one with her (Eph. 5:31). Becoming one with your spouse involves being devoted to his or her well-being. You must envision yourself meeting all of your spouse's natural and physical needs. You must commit yourself to paying close attention to those needs daily. Further, you must become convinced that tending to the needs of your spouse will enrich your own life. Often in premarital classes, I advise couples to focus especially on pleasing their spouses in the area of sexual intimacy. If you will serve your spouse in this area, and you marry someone who will serve you, then you have nothing to fear.

"But what about those of us married to people who really don't care about pleasing us?" you ask. You must set an example for your spouse and reflect what God intends for your marriage. By the irresistible grace and love you demonstrate, you can win your spouse to you and replenish your relationship.

Here are some practical things you and your spouse can apply as you learn to serve one another in fresh ways.

Survey One Another

Ask hard questions like, "What can I do to please you more?" If we would only take the initiative, we could help our spouses overcome their difficult issues. Frequently, we address our spouses' feelings only when we know something is wrong. Such moments aren't typically conducive to intimate communication. If we ask probing questions in less confrontational settings—on a date or in the moments after sexual intimacy—then we are much more likely to get desirable responses.

Later I'll address in detail the importance of dating your spouse in a purposeful, consistent way, but let me share this now. Too often we fail to listen to the heart of the person we've married. Marriage is not a fairy tale or a Hollywood production. Great discussions don't occur out of the blue. You must plan to spend time together in low-stress situations so that your thoughts and feelings have a chance to arise naturally. Here is a list of questions to get you started:

1. What can I do to make you feel loved and appreciated?
2. Do you have any fears that consistently haunt you?
3. Are there specific times when you need me to be more sensitive to your feelings?
4. What would you like your life to be like in ten years?

Never underestimate the power of knowing what your spouse thinks and feels about the issues of life. Again, you will not come to these discussions without planning. Determine to spend time together with no agenda other than being in one another's company. You'll be surprised by the interesting discoveries you make.

Finally, you gain more insight about each other during conflict than at any other time. Learn from disagreement and discuss what you've gleaned once you're in a relaxed environment.

Compliment One Another Often

A wise partner can bring his or her spouse's unique and wonderful qualities to the surface by speaking words of compliment and kindness. Yet to our own detriment, we seem to miss opportunities to edify our loved ones, while we seize opportunities to ridicule or criticize them. All of us have been in the presence of people who spew out so many derogatory remarks about their spouses—it's a wonder they ever got married! When my wife, Janeen, and I were in premarital counseling, our pastor challenged us never to say anything negative about one another in public—not even in jest.

Over the years, this practice has become one of the most powerful deterrents in our marriage to insensitivity and insecurity.

You and your spouse can lay the groundwork for encouragement in your marriage by revisiting your courtship. After years of dealing with financial challenge, children and all the other things that make life authentic, we can forget about the qualities that originally drew us to our spouses. Return to those qualities in your mind. Begin to see your spouse in that original light. Tell your husband again what you find attractive in him. Share with your wife how much you value the unique aspects of her nature.

If your husband or wife insists accolades are unnecessary, don't believe it for a minute! Words build people up. That's why God spends so much time telling us in His Word that He loves us and has good plans for us. He knows we need to hear encouragement spoken in a personal way. Where would you be today without your Bible, God's encouraging message to you? Don't leave your spouse without a declaration of how special and wonderful he or she is in your eyes.

Someone may ask, "Do I need to be specific?" Absolutely! Don't speak in generalities. The men at your wife's job can tell her general things they appreciate about her, but you create a place in her life no one can duplicate when you assert in detail what you love about the way God made her. Other women may recognize your husband's obvious attributes, but you have the inside track. Use that information to build him up; speak highly of the man you fell in love with.

Learn As Much As You Can About Your Spouse's Greatest Desires

Do you know what your wife longs to accomplish in her lifetime? Can you share the deepest dream of your husband's heart? You may be able to answer affirmatively now, but you must take a "continuing education" approach to your spouse's aspirations.

Once you become acquainted with your spouse's deep desires, you'll be able to do three important things more effectively:

1. Pray for your partner in specific terms.
2. Encourage your spouse with understanding.
3. Release your husband or wife to become what God has ordained him or her to be.

When people enter midlife—or their "second adulthood," as Gail Sheehy, the author of the best-selling book *Passages*, aptly calls it—they may begin to ask themselves whether they've accomplished anything of value. Marriages can come under strain in such seasons. Your spouse may begin to doubt his or her worth. If your wife fears that you, her closest confidant, don't understand her deepest longings, then your relationship will suffer. You can't please your wife until you know what pleases her.

What pleases a person is intimately tied to the thing he or she longs to achieve in life. Early in our marriage, my wife became an excellent seamstress. She had always exhibited talent in fashion design, but I must admit, our limited finances forced her to become increasingly innovative. In time, I learned my wife wanted to use her gifts to design a line of clothing Christian women could wear proudly without succumbing to the world's fads. I decided to help in every way possible. I trusted God for the money to purchase a small, used sewing machine. Then I helped Janeen rent a hall for her first fashion show. I even did some of the modeling and commentary. Years later, I was able to help her open a boutique and even sent her to New York to buy the clothes for it. Mind you, I have no personal interest in promoting fashion—what I'm interested in are my wife's hopes and dreams.

Notably, my involvement in Janeen's vision has enabled her to better handle my own demanding schedule. I have proven to my wife that I care about her aspirations. She, in turn, doesn't feel threatened by the activities and people that often require my energy. What's more, I draw energy from her support. My wife's interest in my destiny has been the greatest inspiration in my life. No one understands better what the Lord has called me to do and how important it is to me that I fulfill the call. Janeen has taken on numerous responsibilities just because I believed we needed to do so. She frequently asks how I feel about the ministry's direction, an academic course I'm taking or a message I've preached. I don't know whether she's that interested, but she sure makes me feel good when she asks.

Determine to understand your wife's direction better than anyone she will ever meet. Resolve to have a clearer picture of your husband's purpose than anyone in the world.

Heavenly Father, help me to consider my spouse before I think of myself. Don't allow me to operate selfishly in this relationship, but help me to give my best. Teach me to give out of a love for both You and my spouse, regardless of whether I get anything in return. I desperately need Your help in order to live this way. Show me how to be like You—a servant. In Jesus' name, amen.

CHAPTER 2

Remove the Word *Divorce* From Your Vocabulary

Build Protection From Insecurity

Drastic times deserve drastic measures.

I f God is at work in our lives and He hates divorce, why should we ever use the word? Actually, *divorce* comes from the Latin word *divertere*, from which we get our word *divert*. To divorce is legally to dissolve a marriage. Considering the Latin root, we could argue that to divorce is legally to divert a marriage—or to remove a marriage from its original course.

God's Message Through Marriage

God designed marriage to illustrate Christ's love for the church. As individuals, we may fail and even walk away from fellowship with Christ, but He will never divorce the church, His bride. The love of God endures all things, it is patient and kind, and it never fails. (See 1 Corinthians 13:4–8.) When a man commits his life to his wife and a woman her heart to her husband, they present an image of God's eternal, self-sacrificial devotion to His people. To break our marriage covenant through divorce is to ruin the picture of love that God created for a dying world.

Our Children Suffer in Divorce

Our children should provide reason enough for us to banish divorce from our marital conversation. No matter how you may justify failure in marriage, children suffer deeply when their parents break covenant. Children of divorced parents will wrestle with excessive insecurity, and they will have difficulty loving for fear of being hurt themselves. When parents drag their children through mean-spirited court battles, the result is often emotional damage from which it takes the children years to recover. Some studies show that children reared in broken homes themselves are more likely to become divorced.

If you are a child of divorce, don't be afraid. Your marriage isn't doomed to failure. With God's help, you can overcome whatever emotional obstacles you face. Remember, when you are in Christ, old things pass away—all things become new (2 Cor. 5:17).

Divorce: A Last Resort,
and Only in Certain Cases

We balk at the world's ever-increasing divorce rate, but the truth is, without Christ it proves exceedingly difficult—and in some cases impossible—to love unconditionally. What should set church leaders on edge is that divorce has become just as frequent among Christians as among non-Christians. Regrettably, many Christian leaders have compromised their teaching about divorce and remarriage precisely because these phenomena are common in the church.

I will tell you what many leaders hesitate to say: Other than sexual unfaithfulness, physical abuse or desertion, I am convinced there are no grounds for a Christian to divorce his or her spouse and marry someone else. Even when one or more of the above-listed sins seems to have destroyed a marriage covenant, divorce should be considered the last resort. In our ministry, for instance, we've found that God does not always release a person from marriage after his or her spouse has been unfaithful. Rather, the Lord may give the wounded spouse the love needed to forgive and seek reconciliation. Because every situation is unique, you should only proceed with divorce in such cases after praying earnestly and seeking pastoral counsel.

If you are one who has betrayed your spouse in any of the areas named above, then recognize that you effectively have trampled underfoot the gift of trust God imparted to you when you married your husband or wife. You have broken covenant with your partner and put great strain on the relationship. While severe damage of this sort can be overcome with much counsel and prayer, prepare to work hard and endure difficulty. Repent to your spouse, take steps to change your behavior and seek counsel right away.

Some may consider this an extreme or narrow

approach to the subject of divorce, but I argue that drastic times deserve drastic measures. If you already are divorced and remarried, then make a decision to remain faithful in your current relationship. Divorce may have been your only alternative in your earlier marriage, or you may have divorced a previous spouse without biblical grounds. Either way, you must commit to removing the word from your vocabulary now. This is a new day.

Take the Divorce Card Off the Table

Married couples must resist the temptation to use the threat of divorce to get the upper hand during difficult times. Many people live daily with the fear of losing their spouses. Heated discussions about divorce only stir that fire. Don't give the enemy a card he can play at his leisure. If you carry the divorce option up the proverbial sleeve, then you'll eventually be forced to play it. On the other hand, you can't play a card you don't possess. If you have ever used threat of divorce as a weapon, go to your spouse and repent before reading any further in this book! Assure your spouse that divorce is not an option for you. You will deal a deathblow to insecurity in your relationship as a result.

I often tell my wife, "If you want to get rid of me, you'll have to kill me." While I'm sure the thought has crossed her mind over the years, I'm alive and married today by the grace of God.

Once divorce is no longer an option in your own marriage, amazing things will begin to happen for you and your spouse. You will be free to love fully!

Heavenly Father, today I decide to remove the word divorce *from my vocabulary. Whatever has happened in the past, I release it to you; I determine to forgive my spouse with the help of the Holy Spirit. Prevent me from using the threat of divorce against my spouse or even considering divorce as an alternative. I commit myself to a prosperous, enduring marriage with my spouse until we are separated by death. Thank You for establishing covenant love between us. In Jesus' name, amen.*

CHAPTER 3

Show Affection Daily

∽

Maintain Unity, Demonstrate Acceptance

Once you decide to be affectionate, you'll enjoy the results so much you'll want to be more affectionate!

One of the missing elements in marriages today is the outward demonstration of love we call affection. When we see couples holding hands or kissing in public, we likely assume, "They must be dating," or "They're probably newlyweds!" It's unfortunate but true: We don't often associate affection with a long-term marriage. The entertainment industry doesn't help matters. Movies seldom portray marriage as exciting or passionate. In most Hollywood productions, only adultery or sexual interaction outside of marriage evokes the kind of ardor our marriages desperately need.

Affection carries greater emotional and psychological value than many people understand. Studies show that babies who receive love and affection become healthier children, both physically and emotionally, than neglected infants. We are no different. You and I have a deep-seated need for affection. And so do our spouses.

As married people, our challenge is to keep the flame in our marriages alive. After years together, we tend to become so familiar with our spouses, and vice versa, that we lose the "mystique" of affection and sexual attraction. Once this happens, our relationships become especially vulnerable to attack. Our spouses may feel devalued, as if they are no longer attractive or important to us. The antidote in such cases, you will find, is affection.

"I'm Not the Affectionate Type"

While it is true some people tend naturally to be more affectionate than others, it is not true that people less inclined to physical warmth have to stay that way. As we've learned, marriage is only successful when we devote ourselves to pleasing our spouses. Part of pleasing our loved ones involves showing them affection. In other words, affection is part of the package. It's not optional. Therefore, we must determine to give love in this way.

Here's the good news: Once you decide to be affectionate, you'll enjoy the results so much you'll want to be more affectionate! You may discover that reading books about affection will help you get started.

Whatever you need to do to gain inspiration, do it. If you truly love your spouse, you will work to meet his or her need, no matter the cost.

Talk About How Much You Love Each Other

Affection isn't limited to physical touch. Words too can convey affection. In fact, when a marriage lacks physical love, it likely lacks verbal love. You can restore an atmosphere of warmth to your marriage by starting with language. Share with your spouse the things you love about him or her. If you struggle with communicating your feelings at first, then purchase greeting cards that express what you would like to say. Your spouse will appreciate the effort you've made, and you will be encouraged to continue. As a matter of fact, you may want to buy several cards and send one to your husband or wife every week. If you can sing or write poetry, then use these forms of communication to release words of affection to your spouse. Sure, you may be embarrassed a little, but don't give up!

Expressing affection not only infuses our marriages with a new measure of emotional health, but it also benefits our children. First, you'll find that as you become more adept at giving verbal love to your spouse, you'll become more verbally affectionate with your kids. Second, when you speak affectionately to your spouse, you instill a powerful standard for marriage in your children's hearts. Imagine the trans-generational impact you can have by making the decision to love your spouse with your words.

Touch Each Other Daily

Surprisingly, we often assume good habits in our marriages come naturally. Time proves us wrong again and again. We must plan to do things! When you rise in the morning, make plans to touch your spouse at least once that day. Never let a day go by when you don't extend physical love to your spouse. A hug or a kiss regularly will keep feelings of acceptance burning in both of your hearts.

I often suggest to the couples in our church that whenever they leave one another for any significant period of time, they kiss each other good-bye. The truth is, people die while going to the grocery store or to work. What better memory than a kiss if we must be separated from the one we love. I'm not suggesting we should live expecting tragedy—rather, we should live each moment as if it were our last. Over time, we will better appreciate our spouses and become less inclined to take one another for granted.

Break Old Patterns of Neglecting Affection

I challenge you to examine your relationship and determine how much work you need to do in order to give your spouse adequate affection. If it has been your habit to rarely touch your spouse outside of sexual relations, then take steps to change. If you don't, that pattern over time will destroy whatever semblance of intimacy remains in your marriage.

Here are a few questions to ask yourself:

- When was the last time my spouse and I held hands?

- How often have I kissed my spouse this week?

- Did I kiss my spouse the last time one of us drove away?

- Would our kids think of us as affectionate? (My kids often walk by their mother and me showing affection and say, "Get a room!" We reply, "We have one!")

- Does my spouse consider me affectionate?

You may not realize it, but affection is as significant an ingredient as any other in a successful marriage. Please don't treat affection as optional. While you may not be comfortable showing affection at this point, don't consider warmth something reserved only for romantic people. Your spouse, like everyone else, needs affection. If you tell yourself otherwise, you're fooling yourself. Realize that if your spouse doesn't get attention and affection from you, he or she will likely seek it elsewhere: from a career, shopping, the children or the worst scenario—in the arms of another! Don't let that happen. Take control of the temperature of your marriage. Be affectionate!

Heavenly Father, I commit myself to meeting my spouse's need for affection, and I ask You to help me demonstrate love with consistency. If I have failed my spouse in the past, then please show me how to repent and improve. Cancel the influence of anything from my background that prevents me from showing my spouse the affection he or she deserves. Let my spouse sense Your love in my heart, see Your concern in my eyes, hear Your love in my voice and feel Your love through my hands. In Jesus' name, amen.

CHAPTER 4

Make Love Regularly

⌒

Honor God's Word, Build Intimacy

If you're riding down the road in a newly purchased Rolls Royce, you're not going to be tempted to steal a 1968 Volkswagen from someone else. Make your sexual relationship with your spouse a Rolls Royce relationship.

The church has always battled to separate itself from worldly perversion, but we may have gone too far in some areas. Sexuality is one of them. Faced with today's sexual excesses and distortions, we subtly teach believers that sexuality is negative; we condemn sexual activity without bringing balance to the discussion through the Word of God. We overlook what God says about sexual love.

Sexual Love Is the Plan of God, and It Is Good

The writer of Proverbs offers a very clear—and uncomfortably specific—exhortation about the blessing of sexual love.

> Let your fountain be blessed,
> And rejoice in the wife of your youth.
> As a loving hind and a graceful doe,
> Let her breasts satisfy you at all times;
> Be exhilarated always with her love.
> —PROVERBS 5:18–19

Notice the writer tells his young reader to rejoice with the *wife* of his youth—not the girlfriend or weekend fling of his midlife crisis! God meant sexual love to be enjoyed by monogamous couples united in lifelong covenant. In stressing its parameters, however, let's not miss out on the exuberance of sexual love. The Word says to be blessed, rejoice, be exhilarated! We should be enthusiastic about sharing ourselves physically with our spouses. If we are not, then let's commit to doing whatever is necessary to regenerate this aspect of intimacy in our marriages. Otherwise, we leave an open door for temptation.

God's original intent was that sexual love would provide:

- A means for procreation so that men and women could produce after their own kind.
- A healthy way for men and women to meet one another's deepest needs.
- An intimate form of recreation that is both

physically exhilarating and emotionally comforting for husband and wife.

We know from the creation story in Genesis that God put His divine stamp of approval on everything He made by saying, "It is good." This is true of sexual intimacy, too. God made it; therefore, it is good.

"If Sexual Intimacy Is Good, Then Why Am I Suffering?"

Trauma from sexual intimacy prior to or during marriage is not uncommon. In such circumstances, both spouses need to work together with the Lord to bring healing to deep-seated wounds. It may prove helpful at this time to examine some ways that you and your loved one can address physical and/or emotional injury.

Childhood abuse

My wife and I frequently counsel people who as children were sexually abused. Sexual abuse for a woman can range from being touched inappropriately by a relative or "friend" of the family to actually being raped by a man who may or may not be part of the family. In many cases, we find that women have suffered abuse at the hands of both men and women. Men who have been molested usually deal with abuse that is homosexual in nature, making it difficult for them to confront the trauma, let alone heal from it.

The "pressure" of sexual intimacy in marriage often further complicates what is already an intricate set of wounds. A woman, for instance, may convince herself she'll be able to enjoy sexual intimacy in marriage, only to discover the old injuries are too deep and too complex to suppress. The guilt of not being able to meet her husband's sexual needs only compounds the problem. On the other hand, men—already overstressed by the issues ensuing from past sexual abuse—may find themselves doubly burdened by the complex sexual needs of their wives.

For those of you who have faced abuse as children or teens, your freedom will come as you are able to talk about what you have experienced. Share with a spiritual leader or counselor and allow the Lord to begin the process of healing. Talk to your spouse. Assure your husband or wife that your inability to demonstrate sexual love at this time does not reflect a lack of desire for him or her.

The most difficult but most rewarding task will be finding it in your heart to forgive the person who victimized you. In this way, you can put the trauma behind you. The Holy Spirit graciously will cause you to forget the pain and anguish, and He will produce a vibrant, loving relationship between you and your spouse.

Sexual activity before marriage

Not all of the sexual activity we experienced outside of marriage was forced upon us. Some of the problems we face in marriage stem from voluntary, premarital sexual activity. The key to overcoming our difficulties on this front is to confess our sins to God. Once we confess and receive forgiveness, past sins lose their authority in our lives. We may wrestle from time to time with guilt, but if we stand confidently upon God's promise to forgive, then the guilt will pass.

If you were sexually active before marriage and have not already asked for forgiveness, then take the time now to do so. Admit your sin to God and ask for forgiveness and cleansing. Ask the Holy Spirit to remove from your life any effects of past sexual sin. Honor the needs of your husband or wife, and commit yourself to being faithful to one person until you are separated by death.

Negative sexual experiences in your marriage

Many people wait patiently and refrain from sharing in a sexual relationship until marriage. Unfortunately, they may find themselves married to spouses who don't understand how to meet their sexual needs. This kind of incongruity can put a great deal of strain on a marriage. Don't assume that satisfying sexual relationships come naturally. If you have not been properly prepared through reading, teaching and effective counsel, then you will struggle in this area of intimacy. To lay the foundation for a fulfilling sexual relationship with your husband or wife, you first must acquire a healthy awareness of the sexual differences between men and women.

Sexual Differences Between Men and Women

Both spouses should carry the responsibility for meeting the sexual needs of the other as required by God's Word: "Let the husband fulfill his duty to his wife, and likewise also the wife to her husband" (1 Cor. 7:3). Yet as men and women, we must recognize our psychosexual responses tend to differ. We are not sexually aroused by the same things or at the same pace. Often we don't find the same aspects of sexual encounters satisfying.

For instance, men tend to become aroused by what they see and women by what they feel. No wonder men are addicted to pornography at an astronomically higher rate than are women. Pictures just don't do much for most women. By contrast, women who fall into adultery often testify that what first tempted them was not physical attraction to another man, but the way the man made them feel inside.

As a wife, satisfying your husband is less complicated than your husband's task of satisfying you. Someone reportedly once asked a famous movie actor, "What does a woman have to do to turn a man on?" He replied, "Just show up!" If you will show up beautifully prepared for your time of sexual intimacy with your husband, demonstrate a loving attitude and respond positively to him, then you will succeed in meeting his needs and building his self-esteem.

You can increase your husband's confidence further by initiating sexual relations from time to time. Leave him a note encouraging him not to stay at work too late or at the computer too long. Your initiative will signal to your husband that you are happy to be in a sexual relationship with him. This greatly diminishes the influence of temptation in the life of a man.

Husbands, on the other hand, need wisdom and determination if they are going to meet their wives' sexual needs. Christian women in particular tend to downplay their needs and, as a result, are among the most sexually frustrated women in the world. Often they are taught, directly or indirectly, that their own sexual fulfillment doesn't matter. "Honey, you just take care of your man so nobody else will," goes the familiar saying. Add to this mind-set the fact that most churches lack adequate premarital training for couples—not to mention open discussion about sexual issues—and you can understand the difficult place many married Christian women inhabit. A one-sided approach to sexuality was never God's intent. The Lord designed sexual relations to be a two-way street—a dialogue, not a dead-end monologue.

Men must be kingly and pursue their wives' sexual passions with tenacity. A woman may express her passions less obviously than a man, but make no mistake: Those passions are there. Early in my relationship with my wife, I discovered the time spent prior to actual lovemaking was essential to her enjoyment. As a man, I had to learn to resist the temptation to move from phase to phase too quickly, and my wife had to learn that sexual patience was a virtue I would not be able to acquire instantly!

Husbands also must learn to employ a gentle touch throughout foreplay. Allow your wife to educate you about her desires and inform you of her readiness for intercourse. Once you've convinced your wife that you are carrying a burden to see her fulfilled in sexual intimacy, her attitude toward both you and lovemaking will change.

Build a Rolls Royce Relationship

If sexual intimacy has been a struggle for you and your spouse, repent of your lack of understanding today and begin to make plans to improve. Schedule a weekend getaway to jump-start your intimacy. More importantly, commit yourself to investing regular time in your sexual relationship with your spouse. The more you make love with an earnest attitude to please one another, the closer you and your spouse will become and the more you will desire each other. Here are some strategies to help you create the Rolls Royce relationship God desires you to have:

- Develop a romantic atmosphere by using candles, soft music and preferred colognes and perfumes. Ensure you have complete privacy.
- Purposely take your time during foreplay and learn to express love through intimate touch, kind words and a gentle kiss.
- Husband, allow your wife to guide your actions and set the pace.
- Wife, encourage your husband by affirming his attempts to please you and taking the lead now and then.

When the Word of God instructs men and women to meet the sexual needs of one another, it pictures the Lord's broader desire: that we put down lasting foundations in all areas of our marriage relationships. In other words, the beauty of creating a vibrant sexual relationship with your spouse has much to do with the benefit such intimacy brings to other aspects of your marriage. Believe me, the enduring fulfillment in your married life is worth all of the time and effort you spend nourishing your sexual life.

Heavenly Father, while it seems awkward to talk to You about my physical relationship with my spouse, I recognize my need for Your guidance. Help me to satisfy my spouse's sexual needs and desires. Teach me to focus on pleasing my spouse instead of being pleased. Lord, I confess any failure in this area of my life and receive Your forgiveness. I also receive Your healing for any sexual brokenness in my life. Let the romance and passion in our marriage burn brightly all the days of our lives together. Thank You for teaching us to prosper in the area of sexual intimacy. In Jesus' name, amen.

CHAPTER 5

Plan to
Get Away

∽

Renew the Flame!

Even a hot fire will go out without sufficient
fuel and attention.

I n today's world, "burn out" is a mundane experience. People burn out at work. They burn out at
home. They burn out at church. Marriages burn out
and are doing so at an excessive rate. In fact, marriage
and child-rearing are two of the greatest sources of
stress in America. If you don't refuel your marriage on
a regular basis, you'll set yourself up to quench what
should be your greatest source of blessing.

Fueling your marriage amounts to spending time
with your spouse. Whatever your calling in life, you
and your spouse need time away from daily pressures
to focus on one another. Once you dedicate yourselves

to prioritizing this time together, you'll notice increased refreshment in your life. Your physical and emotional health will improve. Sexual intimacy with your spouse will become more satisfying. Your spiritual life will deepen.

A Three-Part Plan

Throughout our marriage, my wife, Janeen, and I have practiced spending time together according to the following plan, and our marriage has flourished through periods of strain that otherwise would have significantly frayed our relationship. We are grateful to those who taught us the value of regular getaways, and we've attempted to teach this principle to the people we lead.

By the same token, when Janeen and I fail to spend time together as we've committed, we pay for it. Perhaps we allowed the pressures of ministry or raising children to keep us from escaping with one another on a regular basis. Regardless, the unpleasant repercussions of those decisions have helped us realize that we are much better parents and pastors when we are refreshed in our relationship.

Set aside a weekly date time, and commit not to alter it except in emergencies.

Jesus never married, but He did enter into covenant relationship with His disciples. Their travel schedule was hectic and the weight of ministry great. Yet Jesus found time to spend with His disciples in fellowship and prayer. They didn't just perform miracles together; they went to dinner together. In short, they relaxed together.

You need to do the same with your husband or wife. Consistently dating your spouse is one way to keep fatigue, irritation and loneliness out of your relationship. Once you set a regular date time, you will begin to look forward to it. Life can drain us, and time with our best friend will help lift our spirits. Your dates will become the soil out of which new intimacy is produced in your relationship.

Weekly dates help us remember what attracted us to our spouses before we married them. An evening walk together, a wholesome movie or a dinner date gives us the opportunity to experience the wonderful qualities that drew us to our spouses in the first place. When I counsel couples who are adrift and discouraged in their marriages, I often ask, "If your husband is that terrible, then why did you marry him?" Or, "If your wife is so bad, then why did you ever propose?" I find that people have trouble answering these fundamental questions, which points to the smothering power of life's difficulties. Weekly dating will help us guard the most precious aspects of our marriage relationships.

When you make dating a priority, you bolster your spouse's sense of security in the relationship. You do wonders for your wife's self-worth when you turn down a basketball invitation with your buddies to keep your weekly date. If your husband knows you won't even consider a dinner invitation with your women friends because it conflicts with your date time, then his confidence level will rise.

Most of us have heard the adage, "The family that prays together stays together." I must tell you that I know some Christians who claim to have prayed with their spouses and are now divorced. I don't know any couples, however, who experienced divorce or separation while faithfully dating one another. The point, of course, is to do both—pray and date.

Take a weekend together every three to four months.

The previous section may have posed a sizeable challenge to many of you, but this section will prove even more daunting. While difficult to schedule, a weekly date doesn't have to cost much. (The date can be an ice cream cone at a fast-food restaurant!) A weekend with your spouse is another matter. Not only must you and your spouse work to schedule the excursion, but you must also sacrifice to afford it.

Your marriage needs a breather every quarter. You can arrange a spontaneous expedition to a campground or a well-planned overnight at a five-star hotel, but you must get away with your spouse for at least forty-eight hours. Money and time cannot become excuses to carry on with the status quo. In fact, some of the blessing you experience as a result of getting away corresponds directly to the resources you put into the trip. You bestow value upon one another when you and your spouse go on a weekend together.

The Bible says God loved us so much He sent His only Son to die for our sins. (See John 3:16.) Many people in today's world suffer from a feeling of worthlessness. You may have experienced this kind of despair at times in your own life. One of the keys to freedom from low self-esteem is understanding just how highly God esteems you. God knew you and had a purpose for your life before you were conceived. The Lord Himself placed you in your mother's womb. You are no accident. Not only did He create you, but He also loved you so much that He died for you. The Holy One, the King of kings, died so that you could be clean in His sight and draw near to Him in relationship. He wanted to be with you that badly. Once you grasp the power and depth of God's love for you personally, once you comprehend even a fraction of how much He values you, your own capacity to value and esteem yourself will expand.

Even as God assigned value to us by paying the ultimate price to save us from the destruction of sin, so we determine the value of things based on what we are willing to pay for them. You may pay a great deal for a house, for example. Or a vehicle. The amount you spend reflects what you think such assets are worth. Consider the same principle when it comes to blessing your spouse. When you invest time and money to get away with your loved one, you assign value to him or her. You must determine, based on your own personal financial condition, what you are able to do for your spouse; but be aware that if you do nothing, you literally communicate that he or she is worth nothing.

Before you dismiss a quarterly getaway as impossible, sit down and examine what you've spent money on over the past month. Of all your expenditures—house, car, clothes, even your children's needs—were any of these purchases more valuable than your spouse? Once you make the quarterly getaway a habit, you'll begin to crave this time of refreshment with your spouse so much you'll love making the sacrifice. The principle, "Give, and it will be given to you," applies at home even as it applies at church (Luke 6:38).

Spend at least one week together on vacation; include your kids on a separate trip.

Every year there are two things my wife and I do without fail. We spend a week together with our kids and a week together alone. Both trips are necessary. If you ever spend five to seven uninterrupted days with your spouse, you will fight to make a lengthy break a part of your annual schedule. The only negative part is coming home. I enjoy the attention of my wife so much, I often begin to feel discouraged the day before we're scheduled to return.

Our family vacation is the highlight of our year. Given the hectic pace children are expected to sustain, they need a vacation, too! Untold numbers of parents are killing themselves to provide for their kids, only to discover their children subtly despise them for never prioritizing family time. People wake up in America every day to find their children grown with no family memories to draw them back home. No photographs from amusement parks. No holiday traditions. Turn on the television, and you'll see the fruit of this state of affairs. Confessional talk shows seem to host an endless stream of guests who are perverted, angry and vengeful because their parents never invested in relationships at home. What a sad commentary on modern life!

It doesn't have to be this way for your family. You can begin today by making a new commitment to spend quality time annually with your children and your spouse.

Here are some practical tips for planning your vacations:

- Talk with your family and/or spouse about desirable vacation spots. Pick a variety of destinations at different cost levels—plan an economy vacation and a deluxe vacation.

- Base your budget on a six- to eight-month savings window, and begin saving right away in order to have enough for transportation, lodging, food and spending money.

- Don't go into debt for a vacation. The bills afterward will kill the trip's effects.

The busier you are, the more you need to sacrifice for a romantic vacation with your spouse. If you are a woman with a demanding career, then your husband needs to be reassured that he is your only love. If you are a man with a taxing schedule and great responsibilities, then your wife needs reminding that nothing you are involved in is more important than she is. An annual trip together will provide you a haven from life's negative consequences and refresh you on your life's journey as husband and wife.

At this point, you may be saying, "A three-part plan for getting away is great, but we'll never be able to do all of this." Don't give up so fast! You can take a step-by-step approach to these habits. Begin with a regular date night each week. Once this becomes part of your routine, you'll want more time together. The quarterly weekend will be just what the doctor ordered. By the end of the year, you'll be longing to get a week away together. Take a cruise, go to Florida, go skiing or camping—but do something for a week with your husband or wife. Over time, you'll experience victories in your relationship that will fuel your desire for more of your spouse.

> *Heavenly Father, lead me as I learn to prioritize time with my spouse. Show me innovative ways to adjust my schedule so that my spouse and I can get away together. Provide whatever we need—sitters, money and time off—so that we can have some days to focus on our relationship. Thank You for teaching me the importance of this principle. In Jesus' name, amen.*

CHAPTER 6

Learn All You Can About Marriage

Leave No Room for Ignorance

My people are destroyed for lack of knowledge.

—HOSEA 4:6

A few years ago I was sharing advice with a well-known gospel singer on how to save his fledgling marriage. I told him that if he wanted to succeed as a husband, then he would have to devote himself to studying two things—marriage and his wife. We've emphasized the importance of knowing your spouse. In this chapter, we'll look at the advantages of knowing some things about foundational marriage principles.

Study to Show Yourself Approved

One thing Americans do well is compartmentalize

our lives, especially in the area of learning. We tend to forego studying once we're out of school. We slack off when it comes to learning because we don't have teachers or deadlines hanging over our heads. We consider ourselves free of the tediousness and exertion we may have experienced in high school, college, technical school or graduate school.

But the Word of God tells us that freedom is tied to knowledge—knowledge of the truth. Jesus said, "If you abide in My word, then you are truly disciples of Mine; and you shall know the truth, and the truth shall make you free" (John 8:31–32).

The apostle Paul understood the power of knowing God's Word. He admonished his young disciple, Timothy, to study the Word as a worker works at his labor. "Be diligent [study] to present yourself approved to God, as a workman who does not need to be ashamed, handling *accurately* the word of truth" (2 Tim. 2:15, emphasis added).

How many times have you blown it in your marriage because you've made an inaccurate decision? As your own experience may prove, ignorance in marriage is hardly bliss. Unfortunately, because we assume marriage will come naturally, we often wait until the bottom falls out in our relationships before we realize the only thing we do naturally is sin.

The Bible puts it this way: "There is a way which seems right to a man, but its end is the way of death" (Prov. 14:12). As you give yourself to understanding God's principles for marriage, you will learn to stop doing what *seems* right and begin consistently to do what *is* right!

Read As Much As You Can About Marriage

Readers make leaders. This is a saying familiar to many young people, but it needs to become familiar to us married folk, too. If we can read, then we can lead. More than twenty years ago, my wife and I began studying in preparation for marriage. Our pastors taught us we needed to purchase books on the subject and apply the knowledge we received. Since then, learning for us has become a habit, and that habit has helped keep our marriage alive and strong. Unfortunately, too many married couples are "flying by the seat of their pants" when it comes to understanding how to walk in God's blessing—and they usually land in the same position!

If you're a man, then please pay particular attention to the suggestions in this section. Satan destroys marriages by keeping husbands in the dark about marital intimacy. Women are the ones who usually purchase and read books about relationships; in contrast, men are the primary consumers of pornography. Considering these trends, we perhaps can draw the following conclusion: Men remain preoccupied with a desire for sexual conquest but are bored by the information that would help them produce genuine sexual intimacy in their marriages.

Men, let's not be duped by our own shortsightedness. Let's invest our time, energy and even our money as we study to improve our marriages. The activity will bring a return so abundant we won't be able to contain it.

41

Here are some practical tips designed especially for male readers:

- Determine to read the Word of God every time you read the sports page or some other secular periodical.

- When your wife suggests you read a book on marriage, see this as God trying to give you information that will produce the kind of relationship you desire.

- Ask your minister to suggest books that have helped develop his or her understanding of good relationships.

- Utilize the resource list at the end of this chapter. It will give you reading material for the next year.

- After you finish this book, read it again, marking the areas of teaching where you need the most improvement.

One of the missing elements in our marriages today is the demonstration of honor. Once you've lived with someone awhile it becomes easy to take him or her for granted. You stop saying "thank you" and "please." You stop opening the car door and cooking special meals. Ultimately, the passion that brought you together erodes. Studying marriage can renew your passion by making your marriage the focal point of your life. As you study marriage, your relationship becomes more important to you—and that change is what produces a fresh sense of honor.

Attend a Marriage Retreat

In the church I pastor, we conduct a marriage retreat every fifteen to eighteen months. I notice the same couples almost always attend the retreat from year to year, and, not surprisingly, these couples rarely suffer serious problems in their marriages. Not only does the instruction at the conference benefit them, but the time away together also brings refreshment to their relationships. Try letting a marriage retreat double as one of your quarterly weekend getaways; you'll come away equipped for deeper levels of intimacy with your spouse.

Impartation and information

Marriage retreats usually serve up a spread of resource materials for those who are hungry for information. Yet whatever spoils you happen to carry away from these retreats, understand you're going to have to do something with the information presented by those books, tapes and videos to get results in your marriage. All the information in the world won't help us if we're not willing to apply what we've received. And applying information takes discipline. Perhaps this explains why at a time when books on marriage abound in the self-help sections of the nation's bookstores, the divorce rate in America is ashamedly high.

Discipline isn't the only thing we need to help us change our attitudes and patterns of behavior. We need the grace of God. Specifically, we need something called "impartation." A preacher can tell us what to do, but each of us also needs the imparted ability to put God's Word into action.

In some Christian circles, believers learn that healing, courage and other spiritual gifts can be imparted through physical touch—what is known as the "laying on of hands." Many things, however, can be imparted from heart to heart. When a preacher shares a word from God, the power to change will be imparted to those who desire to apply and walk in the word. Similarly, as you read this book, you will receive through impartation whatever you need to begin operating in the principles chronicled here.

Your part, as Paul told Timothy, is to give yourself diligently to the task. When Paul urged his young disciple to labor as a workman over the Word of God, he used a Greek word that can be translated as "study." In the original Greek, this word signified more than a pursuit of academic knowledge; it suggested a level of inner commitment that had more to do with determination than intellect. What God really wants is a teachable heart. He wants a man who is determined to learn all he can about marriage and relationship development. He desires a woman who won't give up until she sees results.

Regardless of your educational background, you can make a decision to grow in knowledge for the sake of your marriage whatever the cost. Be wholehearted in this endeavor. Your success has broad implications for you and the generations that follow you. Below you will find a resource list to help you get started.

> *Heavenly Father, there is so much I need to learn about being married. Please teach me from Your Word and lead me to good resources*

so I can nourish and develop my relationship with my spouse. Teach me to read about marriage on a regular basis and learn from the examples of others. Help my spouse and me to learn the joys of a committed marriage. In Jesus' name, amen.

Marriage Resource List

Chapman, Gary. *The Five Love Languages.* Chicago: Northfield Publishing, 1992.

Cole, Edwin Louis. *Communication, Sex, and Money.* Tulsa, OK: Harrison House, 1998.

Shuler, Clarence. *Your Wife Can Be Your Best Friend.* Chicago: Moody Press, 2000.

Smalley, Gary. *For Better or for Best* (for the wife). New York: Harper Mass Market, 1991.

Smalley, Gary. *Hidden Keys of a Loving, Lasting Marriage.* Grand Rapids, MI: Zondervan, 1993.

Smalley, Gary. *If Only He Knew* (for the husband). Grand Rapids, MI: Zondervan, 1996.

Wheat, Ed. *Intended for Pleasure.* Grand Rapids, MI: Fleming H. Revell, 1997.

CHAPTER 7

Give Gifts Consistently

⌒

Add to Your Spouse's Sense of Value

An excellent wife, who can find? For her worth is far above jewels.

—PROVERBS 31:10

While the scripture quoted above compares an excellent wife to precious jewels, the same analogy certainly can be used to describe an excellent husband. When a person finds a loving spouse, he or she has discovered something more valuable than silver, gold or any form of earthly wealth.

What we often fail to recognize is our own ability to increase or diminish our spouse's perceived worth. You actually hold the value of your spouse in your hands. By edifying your wife, for instance, you will cause her to become more valuable in her own eyes—

and thus in your eyes and the eyes of others. When you demonstrate how highly you esteem your husband, he will begin to consider himself more highly. Greater joy will enter his life, and the quality of your lives together as a couple will improve.

In this chapter, we'll discuss gift giving as a way to strengthen our spouses. While financial issues clearly come into play when we consider gift giving, let's remember the thought behind our gift is far more significant than anything else.

Expressing Love and Value

We have no problem devoting time and money to the things we highly regard, a truth we've already examined in the context of planning getaways and vacations with our spouses. From material items like cars and houses to less tangible investments like our children's education, we spare no expense when we are convinced of the worth of our assets. Waxing a car we love, painting a house we plan to die in, polishing silver inherited from parents—whatever the activity: If the object of our attention has value in our sight, caring for it comes easily to us. As a matter of fact, we enjoy tending to our prized belongings when given the opportunity.

Now consider your spouse. Throughout this book, we have assumed as a premise for various arguments that our spouses are valuable; but let's revisit the issue of a spouse's worth. God considers your spouse more precious than anything else He has placed in your life. He loves your spouse so much that He sent His only Son, Jesus, to die for him or her. The truth is, your wife's parents don't realize what a treasure she is. Your husband's boss or closest friend cannot perceive your loved one's hidden value. Just as the bulk of an iceberg remains beneath the water's surface, invisible to the eye, so it is with your spouse's true worth.

Your calling is to expose the concealed beauty of your spouse's inner being. To use another analogy, God placed you in your spouse's life to cultivate and bring to light his or her gifts the way a lapidary brings out the brilliance of a diamond. You, and no one else, are responsible for restoring any luster your spouse may have lost over the years.

What Does a Gift Say?

Noted author and marriage counselor Gary Chapman calls the receiving of gifts a language of love. In his best-selling book, *The Five Love Languages*, Chapman explains that some people view gifts from others as assurances of love and appreciation. Of course, to some extent, everyone enjoys receiving gifts. When someone gives us a gift from the heart, our spirits lift. We feel better about ourselves. If someone spends his or her hard-earned money on us, then we tend to believe we must be worth something.

My wife, Janeen, is a master gift giver. She grew up in a home where giving was a primary love language, and she learned the language well. Recently, for example, I happened to be coping with a great deal of stress due to an increase in ministry responsibilities. The weight of my obligations had become burdensome, and Janeen was well aware of my exhausted condition. During this period, my wife was scheduled to fly to

Florida after an early morning Sunday service to visit our daughter, who was playing in a soccer tournament. As I prepared to say good-bye, my assistant handed me a ticket and said, "You're going, too!" Janeen secretly had executed a plan to give me what I so desperately needed—three days away from ministry in a warm climate with my wife. Did I ever feel special!

The gift my wife gave me spoke volumes about her love for me. Perhaps as impressive as the surprise of the trip itself was what she went through to make it happen. She found speakers to replace me and changed all of my appointments. Because Janeen believed I was worth all of that trouble, I believed I was worth it, too.

Lest you find the link between material transactions and self-esteem carnal or superficial, remember that God Himself honored this very connection. When the Lord wanted to show us how much He loved us, He gave us a gift. That gift was named Jesus.

Create As Many Memories As You Can on Special Days

In developing the habit of gift giving, take full advantage of every special occasion, be it your spouse's birthday, an anniversary, Mother's Day or Father's Day. When you celebrate these days with enthusiasm, you create wonderful memories that will sustain your marriage through times of struggle, sickness and even death.

One particular year, my wife desperately needed something to lift her spirits. Her mother had gone to be with the Lord, and Janeen was suffering greatly from the loss. When our anniversary arrived, I decided to go several extra miles to bless her and came up with the following plan. I arranged for a limousine to pick Janeen up from the house and take her to an undisclosed location. As the limo cruised down a major thoroughfare in our city, my wife noticed a man standing on the side of the road with a sign in his hand. When the car got closer, she noticed something strange: The man was her husband, and the sign read, "WILL WORK FOR LOVE." Needless to say, she was in stitches as I crawled into the limo and took her out for a nice dinner. She will never forget that night.

When you give your energy to showering your spouse with love on special occasions, you not only make memories for your husband or wife, but you also impart blessing to your children. Remember that your example will do more to develop habits in your children's lives than any book or video. By treating your spouse like the treasure he or she is, you strengthen your children for their future marriages by depositing in them certain expectations and desires. What daughter who has seen her father pull out all the stops year after year on her mother's birthday will settle for a man who doesn't value her? What son who has watched his mother surprise his father every Father's Day for decades will find himself with a wife who only loves him half-heartedly?

Keep the Relationship Full of Surprises

Routine often proves an enemy of marriage. When we let our relationships with our spouses become humdrum, we set ourselves up for temptation. After all, the entertainment industry depicts marital infidelity as exciting and adventuresome. Amid such suggestions, a boring day-to-day life with our husbands or wives doesn't help us.

Try spicing things up with your spouse by giving gifts just because you feel like it. When we confine our gift giving to special occasions, our spouses may feel we're giving to them out of obligation. But when we surprise our loved ones with gifts from the heart at random, it does wonders for their sense of value. Get creative, and restore some life to your relationship! By doing so, you can protect your marriage from infidelity and perversion, not to mention improve your romantic life.

Finally, you must take the long view of your marriage. Time has a way of slipping through our hands as we go about our business year after year, but consider your life twenty years from now. What will you remember about your marriage? When you have grown older and your children have families of their own, how will you recall the former days? Will you have memories of birthday dinners, roses spontaneously delivered and lovely cards? Will you remember special days with joy or remorse? Inevitably, you or your spouse will stand over the casket of the other. When that day arrives, will joyful memories overshadow your grief, or will you wish for another chance?

Don't wait too late! Start afresh now. Today is the day to celebrate!

Heavenly Father, thank You for the gift of Your Son, Jesus. Because You gave Him for me, I can be assured that my life has value. Now teach me how to give gifts to my spouse in a way that will build his/her sense of worth. Help me to add flavor to our relationship by giving gifts regularly. Help me to give myself totally to my spouse today! In Jesus' name, amen.

An Invitation

To this point, we've examined marriage principles that anyone—regardless of religious faith—can put into practice. You don't have to be a Christian to attend a marriage retreat or give gifts to your spouse. The book's last five chapters, however, recommend activities predicated on the assumption that you, the reader, have invited Jesus Christ into your life to forgive you, heal you and walk with you as both Lord and friend. Whether or not you choose to make that decision today, please continue to read this book. From time to time you may want to come back to this section and consider your spiritual options.

Here are four principles the Bible teaches concerning your spiritual condition:

1. Everyone is born as a sinner.

In Romans 3:23, we learn that everyone has sinned. Everyone includes you, me and anyone else you can think of. All human beings were born sinners. Being born a sinner does not mean you did something terrible in the womb. To be born a sinner is to be born separated from God. God is a righteous God, and He cannot interact with sin. It concerns Him that you have remained separated from Him all these years; He wants to show you the way into His company.

2. God has a distinct plan for your life.

The Book of Jeremiah explains that God thinks

about you and me. The Lord's thoughts toward us are good and not evil; He wants to give us hope concerning our future (Jer. 29:11). In fact, God created you with something specific in mind. Tied up in His purpose for you is the joy you've been yearning to experience in life. You can actually discover His plan today if you allow Jesus to address the issue of your separation from God.

3. Jesus died to repair your relationship with God.

Romans 5:8 tells us that while we were in our separated condition, Jesus died for our sins. Please understand that God does not hate sinners. The Lord loves everyone. He has always intended to be your friend, so much so that He sent His only Son, Jesus, to take your place on the cross. You see, because we were born sinners, we deserved death. As Romans 6:23 explains, the "wages of sin," or the payment owed for sin, is death. Jesus knew this, and because He loved us, He died in our place. He literally saved us from our sin debt, and thus from death. This is what we mean when we call Him our Savior. Once you accept that Jesus took your sin and paid for it—once you acknowledge, thank and receive Him as your Savior—you will be fully connected to a God who has great plans for your life. You will no longer be separated from the King of kings, who loves you.

4. Today you can ask Jesus Christ to come into your heart, and you can know God.

According to Romans 10:13, any person who calls on the name of Jesus Christ can become a Christian.

That is, we need only admit that Jesus died for us and acknowledge that He is alive today to be saved. We understand that Jesus is alive because after He died on the cross for our sins, the Bible explains that He rose from the dead—He came back to life. The grave could not hold Him; death itself could not kill the life-giving power of God in Christ Jesus. We learn that Jesus walked among His friends and even ate with them after His crucifixion. Then God called Him to heaven.

When you confess that Jesus died for you and rose from the dead, you become a new person. Every sin you ever committed is removed from your life, and you can begin to learn how to follow the Lord daily. If you're a little uncomfortable with how to make that confession to God, then try praying this simple prayer:

> *Dear Jesus, thank You for loving me so much that You gave Your life for me. I admit today that I want new life and a relationship with God, my Father. Come into my heart, and forgive me of all my sins. Make me the person You always meant for me to be. Thank You again for this chance to receive new life and repair my relationship with God. In Jesus' name, amen.*

If you prayed this prayer today, then please write us immediately and allow us to help you as you begin the wonderful adventure of following Christ.

Revival Word Ministries
5847 Poplar Hall Drive
Suite 204
Norfolk, VA 23502
www.revivalword.org

CHAPTER 8

Pray for One Another Daily

⌒

Release God's Power

You become intimate with people you pray for.

Like spiritual bricklayers, you and your spouse can build a wall of protection around your marriage through consistent prayer. Bitterness, unforgiveness, jealousy and discouragement do not easily penetrate a wall of mutual intercessory prayer. When trouble comes, those of you who faithfully pray will find your intercession for one another deflects anger and negativity while releasing the power of restoration. Basically, it's hard to remain irritated with someone you pray for every day!

On the other hand, when you fail to pray for your spouse, you leave him or her—and your relationship—

open to harassment by the devil. In fact, the enemy will work overtime trying to keep you both from praying precisely because your prayers for one another are so vital. Determine to pray faithfully for your loved one whatever your circumstances or emotional condition. As the Word of God says, "Submit therefore to God. Resist the devil and he will flee from you" (James 4:7).

Have a Daily Prayer Plan for One Another

In 1990 the Lord set my wife and me on an odyssey of ministry we never could have dreamed up on our own. That year God called me to leave my position as an engineering manager for a Fortune 500 company in my native Tennessee and move to Norfolk, Virginia, to start a church. We had three children and a fourth on the way. Needless to say, if anyone had a right to be anxious, it was my wife. The move was a daunting proposition in itself, not to mention I had no employment awaiting me, which meant no insurance for the care of the new baby.

Yet the foundation of prayer Janeen and I established enabled us to trust God for our daily needs and to love one another despite the pressure. And God provided every step of the way. We held our first church meeting in our living room with a few adults, their children, a tambourine and a love for God. Twelve years later, we now personally minister to some seven thousand people weekly; our Sunday television ministry reaches thousands across the nation. How did such an explosion happen? How did so much come from so little? While numerous things have contributed to the growth of the ministry and the blessing in our lives, one factor stands out more starkly than them all: *the prayers of a godly wife.*

Since I can remember, it has been the habit of my wife to rise early in the morning and pray. Whatever else may be on her heart or going on in our lives, Janeen begins each day praying for my well-being. The power of her intercession has protected me from sin, helped me generate new ideas and pointed me toward godly wisdom. It scares me to consider where I might be today without the "force field" of Janeen's prayers.

Through prayer, you too can equip your spouse to fulfill his or her purpose in God. The key is consistency and planning. Start by developing a list of areas in your spouse's life you'd like to cover in prayer on a regular basis. Some days you may find you pray about every area on your list; other days you may focus on one or two areas. Regardless, pray daily and, I would advise, at a routine time.

Following are some areas of prayer the Holy Spirit has placed in my wife's heart. You may want to use this list as a pattern for your own intercession. Your husband or wife may not be ministering to thousands in the body of Christ, but he or she is just as significant to God as anyone else. The habit of seeking the Lord on your own for your spouse's wellness and success will bring as great a return in your marriage as praying together. Treat praying for your spouse as your ministry.

- Pray for your spouse's health and protection.

- Pray for your spouse's relationship with your children, his or her coworkers, pastor and relatives.

- Pray for the development of greater intimacy between you and your spouse.

- Pray that your spouse will remain open to the direction of the Holy Spirit each day.

- Pray that your spouse will walk in victory over every temptation.

- Pray that God's Word will be alive and active in his or her daily relationship with the Father.

- Pray that your spouse will be consistent in his or her daily devotions.

Additionally, you may want to pray for your spouse's joy, peace, understanding of spiritual truth, professional success, wisdom in decision making or child rearing, physical health, and faithfulness to God's plan for his or her life. Always pray that God's enabling power and grace will help your spouse meet every challenge he or she faces.

Prayer Can Influence Your Feelings

There is something about calling a person's name before the throne of God that changes our feelings about him or her. It's no wonder Jesus said, "Love your enemies, and pray for those who persecute you" (Matt. 5:44). He knew we would have difficulty not loving the people we carry to Him in prayer. While I trust that your spouse is not your enemy, the same principle can be applied in your marriage. Once you develop the habit of praying regularly for your husband or wife, you will be able to ward off negative feelings toward him or her before those feelings take root in your spirit. If it works for enemies, then imagine the impact on lifelong partners!

Please note: I am not suggesting you replace communication with prayer. If you have an issue with your wife, then both of you need to address it. If your husband offends you, then go to him. Don't take the issue to God. Scripture teaches us to go to the one who has offended us. (See Matthew 5:23–24.) The Lord is not that person! You must go to your spouse and present your grievance before going to God in prayer.

What prayer will do is enable you to keep your heart right with your spouse so that when you must address unpleasant issues, you can do so without malice or destructive anger. Often we fail to communicate in love because we have not prayed fervently for one another. Remember, your prayers are some of your marriage's most effective safeguards!

Prayer Produces Unity

My pastor once explained that those of us who pray will become intimate with the One we pray to, those we pray for and those we pray with. In order to maintain unity, you must spend time not only praying for your spouse, but also with your spouse. The intimacy your prayer time together yields will surpass your expectations; there is nothing like it. Just as we realize what we've missed after skipping days of personal prayer time with the Lord, so it is when we finally pray with our spouses after a season of inconsistency. We experience sweet regret and a desire for more.

For almost twenty years, I suffered under the misconception that praying with my spouse when I could be alone with the Lord was a poor choice. I thought I had to choose one or the other, praying alone with God or praying with Janeen. But during a trip to India, God released me from the tyranny of the "or" by introducing me to the genius of the "and." The choice was not whether to pray with my wife or spend time alone with God; it was to pray with my wife and spend time alone with God. Now Janeen and I try to spend time together regularly praying for one another. Our time with each other does not replace our individual devotional time, but enhances it. As we remain consistent, the intimacy level of our relationship intensifies.

My wife and I have faced many storms over the course of our marriage—storms we likely would not have survived without earnest, consistent prayer. Through the miscarriage of one of our children, the near fatal birth of my son Benjamin, the deaths of our parents and all the ups and downs of ministry, prayer has held us fast.

Praying together means more than praying in the same room at the same time. It means praying for the same things, praying in the same direction and operating as two people who are in covenant with one another. Consider the words of the apostle Peter: "You husbands likewise, live with your wives in an understanding way…and grant her honor as a fellow heir of the grace of life, so that your prayers may not be hindered" (1 Pet. 3:7).

Heavenly Father, thank You that I can communicate with You through prayer. Give me the discipline to spend time praying regularly for my spouse. Stir me to intercede on behalf of my spouse's needs and desires each day. Enable my spouse and me to make time to pray consistently with one another. Draw our hearts together and draw them toward You. Thank You for hearing my prayers for our marriage and family. In Jesus' name, amen.

CHAPTER 9

Repent Constantly

∽

Allow the Holy Spirit In, Keep the Enemy Out

The heart that repents is soft enough to be changed.

Of all the principles discussed in this book, consistent repentance may be the most difficult to practice. As humans, we recoil when it comes to admitting fault or asking for forgiveness. Yet our marriages will flourish only if we regularly address issues and offenses with our spouses. Confronting an issue means confronting the source of that issue. Since our spouses can't possibly be the causes of conflict in every case, we must be ready for the unpleasant business of humbling ourselves and apologizing.

Once we've done that much, we need to determine to change.

Learn to Keep a
Clean Account With God

In the original Greek, *to repent* means "to change one's mind, heart or direction." Jesus explained the principle of repentance in a parable, found in Matthew's Gospel, about two brothers. (See Matthew 21:28–32.) As the story goes, the young men's father asked each of his sons to go and work in his vineyard. One son gave his father attitude, answering, "I will not." But afterward, the Bible explains, "He regretted it and went." The King James Version says the son "repented and went." That is, he changed his direction. He was headed one way, but he humbled himself and turned back.

In contrast, the other son said to his father, "I will, sir," but then he did not keep his word. According to the text, the repentant son is the one who pleased the Lord—not the son who gave a pleasing answer only to back out of his promise, but the son who disobeyed his father and then changed.

A lifestyle of repentance begins with our relationship with God. On a daily basis, the Lord shows us where we need to adjust our thoughts and behaviors. We usually resist these promptings at first. But as we continue to worship God and study His Word, we soften and eventually give in to Him. We understand how desperately we need to change, and out of this revelation comes repentance.

What often keeps us from repenting quickly is our failure to understand our true position as children—sons and daughters—of the heavenly Father. The

Bible teaches us that just like a parent, God corrects those He loves: "For those whom the LORD loves He disciplines, and He scourges every son whom He receives... for what son is there whom his father does not discipline?" (Heb. 12:6–7). When God pricks our hearts about wrong habits or attitudes, He does so because He loves us. He wants us to be whole and healthy; He wants our relationships to be clean and sound. God is not out to get us—He wants to help us! Our part is to let Him.

Learn to Admit When You've Sinned Against Your Spouse

I've stood in front of the mirror of my soul more times than I want to count simultaneously rehearsing apologies to my wife and complaining about having to ask for forgiveness while she gets off the hook. What seemingly supernatural force repels us from all willingness to say those three little words, "Please forgive me"? The force isn't otherworldly at all. It's quite human and commonly known as pride.

Human or not, pride is difficult to ignore. We find it unnerving enough to confess our wrongdoing once or twice; the thought of doing so on a consistent basis at times seems unfathomable. But if we will cultivate an attitude of repentance, we can kick the enemy out of our marriages and make room for the power of the Holy Spirit to enter and heal us.

Recently, my wife and I took a short trip to another city. When we arrived at the hotel, I made a chilling discovery. I had left my wife's suitcase full of clothes sitting on our kitchen floor. I didn't want to be the one to tell her, but I was the only person there. I repented. Her response: "Well, let's go to the mall so I can replace all that you left." What an expensive mistake, you might say. Actually, I was glad to pay for it. Many times in life we discover that a loss we expected to be shattering is easy to recover from. Repentance can't be bought and paid for, but its benefits are worth a great deal. In fact, even the act of repentance usually turns out to be much better than we anticipated.

The best way to win over your pride is to consider the advantages of repentance:

- Repentance breaks down icy communication barriers between you and your spouse.

- Repentance reflects your respect for God, your spouse and your relationship; thus, it enhances the perceived value of your marriage.

- Repentance puts the adversaries of your relationship in a weakened position. If you and your spouse are one, then nothing and no one can come between you.

While you're standing there grumbling over the prospect of saying those three little words to your spouse, keep reminding yourself how much better your relationship will be once you've done it. Things may not improve overnight, but they will improve!

Finally, when you repent to your spouse, be as specific as possible. If you said something that hurt your spouse's feelings, then say, "Honey, it was wrong of me to have made that statement, and I want you to forgive me, please." Nothing is more hypocritical than knowing you've acted inappropriately or spoken unkindly and offering a vague apology like, "If I did anything to hurt you, I'm sorry." My friend, this kind of assertion is not repentant—it reeks of false sincerity. Be an adult; admit what you've done and request forgiveness for the specific wrongdoing.

Don't Let Sin in the Door

Many of us are familiar with the Bible verse that promises, "If we confess our sins, He is faithful and righteous to forgive us our sins and to cleanse us from all unrighteousness" (1 John 1:9). Why delay cashing in on that promise? In fact, when we postpone confessing our sins either to God or our spouses, not only do we sabotage our own blessing, but we also set our relationships up for corrosion.

Consider what you go through when you have an undetected cavity. The decay in the tooth silently spreads until one day the pain in your mouth becomes excruciating. In addition to the pain, you have to endure seriously unpleasant and expensive hours in the dentist's chair to address the damage. So it is with unconfessed sin in your marriage—or in your relationship with the Lord. When left to sit there, sin corrodes your relationship until one day you experience acute pain that costs a great deal more to reverse than it would have if you had repented in the first place.

Beware lest you fall into the ancient response to sin I call "hiding and running." Adam and Eve established the hide-and-run approach, and through the ages, we've made it an art form. After partaking of the forbidden fruit, Adam and Eve looked at one another and hid themselves behind fig leaves to avoid facing the guilt of their sin. Then they began running away from God, whose habit was to meet with them daily. When you experience the same impulse to hide your sin and run from God, remember the Lord wants to forgive you. He longs to see you immediately restored to your rightful place in relationship with Him. Don't run *from* Him—run *to* Him and repent. Do the same with your spouse. You'll be amazed at what God will do to bless and strengthen your marriage!

Heavenly Father, thank You for the gift of forgiveness. Help me to admit when I'm wrong and seek You for cleansing. Teach me the joy that comes from repentance. Help my spouse and me as we learn to repent quickly to one another. Never let us allow unforgiveness to remain in our hearts. In Jesus' name, amen.

CHAPTER 10

Attend Church Together Faithfully

∽

Stay Connected With Others

If you have a church, be faithful—if you don't, find one.

I have a dear friend from Nigeria whose name is Ina Omakwu. He and his wife, Sarah, pastor a large church in the capital city of Abuja. Pastor Ina once said, "After you choose your spouse, the next most important choice you make is where you will go to church." This is a true statement. If you and your spouse are going to fulfill the destiny of God for your lives, then you must link up with a church in your geographical area. The Lord desires for His people to gather together. (See Hebrews 10:25.)

The Bible teaches in Acts 2:47 that as people were hearing the Word of God and believing, or "being saved," they were becoming part of the church. Not

71

just the church in a general sense, but the church specifically located in Jerusalem. Similarly, when you became a Christian, you were born into the world-wide body of believers we call the church. Now you must connect yourself to the local, visible expression of that universal body—an actual church in your city or region.

No Christian is an island unto him or herself. We were designed to work interdependently with other Christians. In particular, God's destiny for you and your spouse is tied to the corporate purpose of the local church you decide to join. You may not find a church overnight, but if you earnestly pray and persist, the Lord will show you where He would like you to put down roots. Part of the Lord's confirmation as to His choice of a church will be your agreement with your spouse. Both of you should experience complete agreement and peace about the decision.

A good church home should meet your needs in the following areas:

- Teaching of God's Word
- Dynamic worship/emphasis on prayer
- Accountability
- Fellowship and friendship

Instruction in the Word

There are thousands of books available on marriage and relationship building, so why is this one helping you? The answer is not the prowess of a profound writer! You are growing because you have located some needed instruction, and you are applying it to your life.

Consider the same principle as you look for a

church home. You should grow as you receive and apply the instruction imparted by a church's leadership. You should see differences over time in your character, your heart and your relationships. These changes constitute the good fruit that everyone plugged in to a local fellowship should experience. Don't misunderstand; life does not become a bed of roses just because you join a church. Rather, the instruction offered by the church should sustain you during difficulty and change you as you endure.

In particular, look for a church that emphasizes marriage and family in its teaching. Does the church include strengthening marriages and families as part of its vision or mission? Look for evidence that the church prizes marriage and family. Do you see some happy families growing in relationship to God and one another?

Worship and Prayer

You and your family need to serve God in a church that understands the true source of His power and the way to His heart. Jesus described such a place in explicit terms: "My house shall be called a house of prayer" (Matt. 21:13). If we intend to please the Lord, then we must worship Him.

Style or musical preference is not the measure for vibrancy in worship. Rather, the attitude of the heart qualifies—or disqualifies—worship before the Lord. When a church believes worship is important, then the congregation will spend time earnestly singing and adoring God. The entire ministry will strive for excellence in praising God and giving Him honor.

Prayer will take place during the service, but more importantly, you will hear prayer discussed frequently as a cherished and vital part of relationship with the Father. Woven into the fabric of such a church's life will be the understanding that accomplishments for God depend not on one's talents and abilities, but on the time one spends before God in prayer.

Accountability

All married couples need friends who can hold them accountable to godly marriage principles. Unless someone outside of your marriage has the right to question you about the relationship, you may find yourself hiding from serious issues in order to maintain the status quo. Avoidance is a very human tendency, but it is one that jeopardizes our relationships with our spouses. As we've noted, sin or conflict allowed to fester in our marriages will only produce a much bigger mess down the road.

A vibrant local church home is the most natural place to build the kind of friendships that will help you keep your relationship clean of negativity and sin. Of course, not everyone in your church qualifies as a potential accountability partner. As God draws you toward individuals or couples, prayerfully and purposefully cultivate those relationships. Make sure the individuals in question are people you trust and respect.

Find couples who are:

- Excited about developing their own marriages.
- Committed to living according to God's Word.

- Willing to share their lives with others.

The premarital counseling my wife and I received from our pastors served to model the interaction we would later need in an accountability relationship. Today, our pastors continue to provide accountability for us. Your accountability partners need not be your senior pastors for the relationship to be effective, but your bond should be built on mutual trust.

God works through accountability relationships often at important junctures. When the Lord began to lead me to plant a church in Norfolk, Virginia, the relationship Janeen and I had built with our pastors gave them the authority to speak into our lives and suggest we wait a year before moving. Knowing the Lord consistently had worked through our pastors to provide wise counsel and direction, we wholeheartedly submitted to their advice. When my wife and I finally arrived in Norfolk in 1990, we felt as if we were players in a theatrical production and had entered on cue. Everything fell into place as the new church began. To this day, my wife and I rejoice that we were accountable to our pastors in formulating our plans.

Learning the Value of Fellowship and Friendship

Individualism is a hallmark American value. Unfortunately, what we call rugged individualism often turns out to be isolationism. We don't want anyone in our business, so we tend to shun the concern of others, often to our own detriment. Incidentally, this mind-set is what makes developing accountability relationships somewhat awkward for us at first.

Our individualistic tendencies also cause us to view regular interaction with others as dispensable or unnecessary. In particular, as Harvard University political scientist Robert Putnam observes in his book, *Bowling Alone*, the percentage of people involved in community and church activities has decreased dramatically over the past few decades. Why is it that our need to work, socialize and strategize with other people seems to be dying?

God's Word teaches that when two or three gather together in His name, He will be there also. In the same text, Jesus says that when we agree on anything, our heavenly Father will do it (Matt. 18:19–20). Should we be surprised, then, that societal forces seem geared toward pulling us apart? No. We must recognize that satan is working to divide and destroy people by keeping them separated.

One way the enemy keeps us from fellowship is by emphasizing past hurts. If you can tell me one story about trying to connect and getting hurt, then I can tell you five. Jesus experienced betrayal, and so do all of us. Don't let a negative encounter at one church keep you from the blessing of fellowship somewhere else. If you've had a bad experience, then learn from it, judge yourself and look for another opportunity to walk in love with others.

Every married couple needs interaction with other people in order to be whole. When isolated from the company of others, we may lean on our spouses for much more than they humanly can or should give us.

While salvation comes to individuals, the life of a Christian is community-based. Jesus died for the sins of the world—a lost community. God so loved the world—a lost community. In order to prosper, you and your spouse must position yourselves in a community.

Fellowship with other Christians in the context of a church home will add a great deal to your life. It allows you to see that others struggle in their marriages, too. It provides you the opportunity to gain valuable feedback from others about the issues you face. Fellowship also gives wives the chance to participate in activities that women may enjoy more than their husbands, and it affords husbands the opportunity to find camaraderie in pursuits that may be of little interest to their wives.

Most importantly, fellowship with others supplies you with encouragement when you are facing trials, trusting God to meet a need or just learning how to pursue God's vision and purpose for your life. God so often reaches us by using people. Through others He assures us we are not forgotten and reminds us that He has the answers to our questions. Place yourself in an active community that God is using for the good of others. Make friends at church—bowling alone is no fun!

> *Heavenly Father, I want to please You by serving in Your house and walking in covenant with Your people. Please help me to be faithful in attending church with my spouse. Even as Jesus enjoyed fellowship with His disciples, show us how to enjoy fellowship with other believers. In Jesus' name, amen.*

CHAPTER 11

Participate in Ministry Joyfully

∽

Release Christ to Others and Blessing to Yourselves

It is more blessed to give than to receive.

—Acts 20:35

I f you are a normal individual, then the first time you heard the above scripture, you flatly disagreed with it. If my mother had told me as a child that all of my Christmas gifts were being donated to the less fortunate—and that I would be blessed by such an act—I would have silently rebelled. No eloquent speeches or promises would have convinced me that having nothing was better than having the things I had asked for.

This type of human self-centeredness, what might be called a grasping mentality, dominates our world—and particularly our nation. People cling fiercely to things, as if their lives depend on what they own. Sadly, many people derive vital aspects of themselves—self-worth, dignity and hope—from their possessions. The life of many an American could be summed up in a financial statement.

Jesus, of course, turned the world's guiding principles upside down. As Paul explained to the Philippians, the Lord's very existence on earth defied the grasping mentality:

> Have this attitude in yourselves which was also in Christ Jesus, who, although He existed in the form of God, did not regard equality with God a thing to be grasped, but emptied Himself, taking the form of a bond-servant, and being made in the likeness of men.
>
> —PHILIPPIANS 2:5–7

Jesus clarified the consequences of the grasping mentality to His disciples: "He who loves his life loses it, and he who hates his life in this world shall keep it to life eternal" (John 12:25). In other words, the secret to a prosperous life in the things of God is letting go. Jesus let go of His life by dying an undeserved death on the cross for our sins. He gave Himself—emptied Himself, in Paul's words—and so must we empty ourselves. Upon this—a life of giving—do our lives and marriages depend.

Get in the Game

When Paul quoted Jesus' words in the Book of Acts about it being more blessed to give than receive, he was talking about the blessing of service—or ministry. Paul was on his way to Jerusalem, where he anticipated he would be arrested. In a farewell address, he told the elders of the Ephesian church to remember that as part of his witness, he had not taken money from the church, but he had worked with his own hands to meet both his needs and the needs of the men who accompanied him. "In everything I showed you that by working hard in this manner you must help the weak and remember the words of the Lord Jesus, that He Himself said, 'It is more blessed to give than to receive'" (Acts 20:35).

Helping the weak, meeting the needs of others— these were the types of activities Paul had in mind when he referred to the blessing of giving. We might read the words of Jesus at the end of the verse this way: It is more blessed to *serve* those in need than to *be served* oneself.

No principle could be more vital when it comes to marriage. As I link arms with my spouse and bless the brokenhearted, feed the hungry or clothe the naked, I am heaping the riches of Christ Jesus upon my marriage. Indeed, as my wife and I go about God's business, He looks after our business. And I would much rather have God meeting my needs than waste time grasping to meet them myself.

All of us have a collection of key memories that undergird our married lives. Here is one of mine: I am seventeen. My pastor from college and I are sitting in our church's small foyer. A beautiful young lady walks by us. Before I can remember to be spiritual, I ask, "Who is that?" I ask the question for several reasons. First, because the young woman is gorgeous; second, because she appears to be about my age; and, finally, because she is leading a group of young people for whom she is responsible in ministry.

By now you've guessed this lovely woman later became my wife. But please understand, God used ministry to bring us together, and He uses ministry to keep couples together. Serving with one another has brought my wife and me great joy and satisfaction for the twenty-plus years we've been married.

When so many advantages can be gained by being involved in ministry together, why do couples fail to make ministry a priority? Life is often difficult, and we become weary. It seems easier to keep to ourselves and look after our own comforts. We grow accustomed to our habits or routines. We don't like change. But by neglecting the opportunity to minister with our spouses, we not only forfeit an entire of level of blessing in our relationships, but we also actually jeopardize our relationships.

I've always had difficulty understanding young, healthy, well-to-do couples who adamantly refrain from having children. As a father of five, my approach to the issue of parenthood is a bit different. My kids have made me the man I am today. (Yes, you can blame them for that!) By giving to them, I've learned the depth and value of God's unconditional love. If Janeen and I had decided to remain childless, what would we have done with our money, time and love? Unless we had found others to bless, we would have consumed God's good gifts ourselves. But because we are called to "minister" to our children, we give everything we have to them. God, in turn, replenishes us.

In the same way, serving in ministry to those in need can keep couples from becoming self-absorbed. Self-centeredness warps your perspective and can erode your relationship. Corporate selfishness as a couple leads to individual selfishness, and when each spouse gets wrapped up in his or her own universe, the marriage buckles. If you and your spouse learn to minister to others, then you will release God's blessings into your marriage in abundance.

In fact, when your own issues seem insurmountable, what you may need is interaction with someone who would love to be in your shoes—the single parent raising her teenagers alone, the widow who just lost her spouse of thirty years, the child suddenly orphaned by the death of his parents. We are called to serve others as Christ, who came not to be served but to be the ultimate servant, served us. If we do not fulfill our God-given purpose—to be like our Savior—then we will not be happy in marriage or in any other pursuit, career or relationship. True joy comes only in the completion of our mission.

Strength in Connecting With Others

Agreement with others for a common purpose releases God's power. The writer of Ecclesiastes refers metaphorically to a rope in order to explain the strength-in-numbers principle: "And if one can overpower him who is alone, two can resist him. A cord of three strands is not quickly torn apart" (Eccles. 4:12).

The point is that when the strands of a rope remain alone, each has a limited measure of strength. But when twisted together to form a rope, the strands increase in strength exponentially. When we and our spouses engage in ministry with others, we effectively form a rope of strength for the purpose of accomplishing the task at hand. Beyond the actual ministry, your marriage relationship will begin to accrue more power on every level as a result of your connection with others. As we've learned, marriage requires involvement in community to succeed. You develop the habit of involvement not just by connecting with others, but also by pursuing common goals with others.

Here are some practical tips to get you started:

- Once you've gotten involved in a church that teaches prayer, worship and the power of the Word of God, search out potential areas of need where you can step in and minister. Choose areas that correspond with your abilities and availability.

- Don't feel trapped because you and your spouse may share different ministry interests. Ministering together does not always mean you and your spouse have to do the same thing in the church. My wife and I never really ministered in the same areas until we began pastoring.

- Find a disadvantaged person who has no association with your church and privately meet his or her need. Locate other charitable agencies of good repute and assist in their work as well. Your ministry should begin in your church, but it does not have to end there.

Give So You Can Give Again!

Begin now to find others you and your spouse can bless. Life was given to us so that we could give it away. Be creative! Take an active stance! I've devoted my life to finding children who need a father, college-bound students who need assistance and struggling folks I can encourage. This is the work that brings me the most joy. Building grand church sanctuaries and preaching to thousands of people are not the endeavors I live for. I live to be a blessing.

Once you begin to share your life with others through ministry, giving becomes a way of life. You enter a wonderful cycle of giving and receiving. You find yourself giving for the joy of giving, not giving to get something back. Over time—as my pastor, Richard Hilton, says—you learn to "give so you can give again!"

God gave us His only Son Jesus that we might live. Giving is His nature; it's what makes Him God. As you and your spouse engage in ministry, you too will take on the heart of giving, the heart of our God.

> *Heavenly Father, today I ask You to show me the gifts You've placed within my spouse and me. Teach us to use those gifts to serve others as we participate where You've called us to minister. Help us to be as committed to blessing others as we are to being blessed. In Jesus' name, amen.*

CHAPTER 12

Build Your Household in Agreement

Invite God's Power

Agree and thrive; disagree and barely survive!

J esus put a high premium on agreement: "Again I say to you, that if two of you agree on earth about anything that they may ask, it shall be done for them by My Father who is in heaven" (Matt. 18:19). With so much authority tied up in agreement, why would we waste our time divided in purpose from our spouses?

Consider the power of common intent as demonstrated in Scripture. When God created humanity, He said, "Let *Us* make man in *Our* image, according to *Our* likeness" (Gen. 1:26, emphasis added). The Triune God—Father, Son and Holy Spirit—agreed about a plan, and that plan was accomplished.

Agreement proves powerful even when plans fail to coincide with the Lord's will. In the era after the

Flood, the people of the earth set out to build a city and a great tower, the top of which would reach heaven. So effective were they in their progress that God had to intervene and frustrate the people's efforts:

> The LORD said, "Behold, they are one people, and they all have the same language. And this is what they began to do, and now nothing which they purpose to do will be impossible for them. Come, let Us go down and there confuse their language, that they may not understand one another's speech."
>
> —GENESIS 11:6–7

God knew disagreement would prove just as destructive for the builders of the Tower of Babel as agreement had proved fruitful. The Word says once God confused the people's language and scattered them throughout the earth, "they stopped building the city" (v. 8). Likewise, disunity in our marriages will hinder our growth and eventually weaken our commitment to our spouses. If we allow disagreement to persist, we may find our marriages hanging in the balance.

For instance, I know the story of a couple who approached their pastor for counseling about a ministry opportunity offered the husband by another church. The man had decided to take the opportunity. His wife totally disagreed. She was kind and respectful, but she didn't believe leaving their church was the right thing to do. Seeing the husband had made up his mind, the pastor decided to focus on the wife's attitude. He encouraged her to follow her husband and trust his judgment.

Sadly, events took a turn for the worse. The

couple's marriage nearly failed, and they ended up returning to their original church to be restored. The husband's decision was not as much the issue as the way he carried it out. He completely disregarded his wife's stance and apparently thought all would be well. Had he prized agreement with his spouse, the devastation could have been avoided.

Develop a Unified Purpose

You and your spouse must promote a vision for your marriage that unites you. By vision, I simply mean your collective goals for home and family. These may include financial, educational and professional goals. We all have plans we want to see come to fruition and milestones we want to achieve. As married couples, we must work to knit these things together so that a good idea does not become a source of division.

In developing a unified vision, both spouses must understand the goals and agree about the timing for their fulfillment. The couple I described in the section above had good ideas. The husband wanted to take on greater responsibility in ministry. What he didn't understand was that his wife's disagreement on timing should have served as a red flag. God often uses our agreement with our spouses as a sign of His involvement. When disagreement arises, we need to pay attention. Never make major decisions in your home until you and your spouse have come to agreement.

Scripture teaches that spouses are to function together as joint heirs of the blessing of salvation. "You husbands likewise, live with your wives in an understanding way, as with a weaker vessel, since she is a woman: and grant her honor as a fellow heir of the grace of life, so that your prayers may not be hindered" (1 Pet. 3:7).

In this passage, the Holy Spirit confirms the equality of husbands and wives who are serving Christ. The use of the word "weaker" to describe women does not signify lower value or diminished intellectual, spiritual—or even physical—strength. My wife had all the babies in our house, so I know which of us is stronger! "Weaker" evokes fragility as might be ascribed to a precious artifact or treasure. Packaging for an expensive vase, for instance, will carry the warning, FRAGILE: HANDLE WITH CARE. The vase is not weak but expensive and in need of proper treatment.

Every husband must be prepared to honor his joint-heir if he has any plans to prosper in his God-given inheritance. The principle of equality in Christ Jesus does not negate a husband's authority to lead in his home. But understand that if you want your prayers answered, then you must walk in agreement with your spouse. Remember, the two of you will inherit the blessings of the Lord together.

Develop a Vision Statement

I counsel married couples to develop a vision statement as a way to ensure they maintain agreement. Agreement is only possible when we share dreams and goals. We may agree completely with our spouses about certain issues or plans but have no idea because we haven't communicated. Articulated agreement will release God's power.

Below is the vision statement my wife, Janeen,

and I use for our relationship. Let it serve as a model for you and your spouse as you develop your own vision statement. Note that a vision statement works as a kind of written legacy for your marriage and family. Your children will be able to read it and remember their parents' commitment to one another. I suggest you keep your vision statement simple. The less complicated your goals, the easier it is to walk in agreement.

Vision Statement for Janeen and Courtney McBath

We envision a marriage in which we walk in complete agreement concerning every significant issue in our lives. We also envision a marriage that will please the heart of the Father and bring Him glory, while strengthening believers and giving hope to the lost. Our marriage will endure the test of time and stand as an example to our children and future generations. We will be true to one another until death.

Pray Fervently to Protect Your Agreement

We've already discussed the necessity of earnest, consistent prayer in marriage. Let me stress here that you should pray on a daily basis for God's hand of protection over your agreement with your spouse. Remember, the enemy comes to steal, kill and destroy (John 10:10). Disagreement or division serves as an open door for the enemy and a prelude to destruction.

The *duty* of protective prayer over our marriages and homes must become a discipline. The *discipline* of prayer must become a desire, and the *desire* must become a *delight*. When this transformation takes place in our spirits, we release the power of fervent prayer to guard our homes from the constant attack of natural and supernatural forces. As Scripture assures us, "The effective prayer of a righteous man [or woman] can accomplish much" (James 5:16).

To maintain our righteousness, or right standing, with God—and thus our effectiveness in prayer—we must resist the temptation to live and act independently of Him. The psalmist wrote, "If I regard wickedness in my heart, the LORD will not hear" (Ps. 66:18). Guarding against personal sin is one of the most powerful ways to protect our prayer lives and thus our agreement in marriage. If we've asked Jesus to cover us with His blood and become Lord over our lives, then we need to let Him be just that: Lord and Master.

Did you know that the command to pray has more to do with God's desire to break our spirit of independence than anything else? Jesus tells us that God knows what we need before we ask Him. God does not need us to pray in order to know our hearts. He asks us to pray so that we won't feel separated from Him. He invites us through prayer to experience a sense of partnership—or agreement—with Him. In prayer we become extensions of God on the earth. When you and your spouse determine to live in agreement with God's principles, you make your home an extension of God's kingdom!

BUILD YOUR HOUSEHOLD IN AGREEMENT

Heavenly Father, help me to develop agreement in my home with my spouse. Give us one vision for our marriage, and help us to commit ourselves to that vision. Lord, we need Your power in order to withstand the attacks against our lives. We thank You now for never leaving us or forsaking us. We stand against the ploy of division and declare that we are one! In Jesus' name, amen.

Conclusion

M y aim in writing this book was to teach you and your spouse how to create basic, life-generating habits in your relationship. Together these habits form a wonderful foundation on which you can build your marriage over time. Once you learn to function in the principles I've explained, you will be positioned to take your marriage to levels you might have thought impossible to attain.

I am praying for you as Paul prayed for the church at Ephesus: "That you, being rooted and grounded in love, may be able to comprehend with all the saints what is the breadth and length and height and depth, and to know the love of Christ which surpasses knowledge, that you may be filled up to all the fullness of God" (Eph. 3:17–19).

Here are some final points to consider as you reflect on what you have learned.

Honor

As I mentioned earlier in the book, many marriages today lack a vital component: honor. We have become so familiar with our spouses that we no longer say good-bye before leaving home; expressions like "thank you," "you're welcome" and "please" have vanished from our conversation. And yet simple acts like opening the door for your wife or sending a thank-you card to your husband produce a great harvest of love and intimacy. Somehow we must recover honor and again learn to operate out of that wild and crazy love we experienced for one another while dating.

Don't kill the spark in your relationship by treating your spouse as if he or she doesn't matter. Guard your marriage by kindling that spark with acts of honor!

Forgiveness

We have not addressed the difficulties couples face as they attempt to forgive one another for neglect, abuse and even infidelity. Many of you desperately want to be on the other side of this mountain. Remember that God teaches, "If we confess our sins, He is faithful and righteous to forgive us our sins and to cleanse us from all unrighteousness" (1 John 1:9).

Forgiveness is a two-part process. First, God forgives or removes our sin from the record He keeps. God forgives because Jesus spilled His blood for us. Our part, simply, is to ask. How great is the grace of God!

Second, the Lord cleanses us from our iniquities as we grow in relationship with Him. "Iniquity" speaks of our tendency toward sin, our inclination to lean in sin's direction. God initially forgives you of the act of sin; the deeper, longer-term work of the Holy Spirit frees you from the inward issues that caused you to commit sin in the first place.

In marriage you will be asked to forgive often, and by God's grace, you will be able to do so. But understand that even as God walks you through a season of cleansing as part of the forgiveness process, so you will have to walk through a cleansing season with your spouse. You may find, for instance, that even after you have forgiven your spouse for something, you hold on to the issue or complaint. God helps us let go of our grievances over time as we allow His Holy Spirit to work in our marriages.

Learn to walk through the entire process of forgiveness. Allow the grace of God to help you forgive your spouse. Then ask the Holy Spirit to cleanse you of all the negative feelings you may be carrying in the aftermath of conflict and hurt.

Work the Book

Utilize this book—let it be a guide, a compass, a measuring stick in your marriage. Don't be overwhelmed by all you've just absorbed. Take each principle one step at a time. When you follow through with any of the habits or activities encouraged here, celebrate with your spouse. Honor your progress together!

If you commit to walking in God's principles, then your marriage can become a sure thing. Let the Holy Spirit produce results through your passionate pursuit of success in your relationship.

A Note to the Men Who Read This Book

For too long our wives have read books on marriage, attended classes on marriage and prayed for our marriages. Unfortunately, many marriage books seek to reach female audiences because women are more likely to purchase books of this kind.

I knew wives would read my book, but I wanted husbands to read it, too. I tried to address men's concerns; I kept the chapters short and concise (my attention span isn't that long either!), and I used myself as an example so that men could relate. Don't let this opportunity evade you! Determine to apply these principles in your daily life.

Finally, as you are the God-called leader in your home, I would like to pray for you:

> *Heavenly Father, thank You for my precious brother. I understand the frustrations we often feel as men, husbands and fathers. I ask that You begin to calm the stormy waters of frustration in his life and release Your peace like a gentle breeze. I pray this man will learn to humble himself before You and his spouse, and that he will lead with love and grace. Together, we repent of our lack of sensitivity toward our spouses and Your Word. Forgive us and cleanse us. We receive the knowledge You have given us and set our hearts to apply these principles daily. Thank You for not giving up on us. In Jesus' name, amen.*

About the Author

Dr. B. Courtney McBath is the senior founding pastor of Calvary Revival Church in Norfolk, Virginia, and the presiding bishop of Calvary Alliance of Churches and Ministries. Since its 1990 inception, Calvary Revival Church has grown to more than 7,000 weekly attendees. Calvary Alliance, established in 1998, includes churches and ministries located in the United States and around the world.

As a pastor and overseer, McBath has committed himself to seeing unbelievers become believers and believers come to maturity in Christ. This commitment is reinforced through his ministries' vision statement: "Building Overcoming Churches Out of Broken Lives Through the Power of Jesus Christ." McBath's work as a prolific speaker, songwriter and author has allowed him the opportunity to share God's Word throughout the nation and abroad. His weekly television program, *The Voice of Revival*, airs nationally on the Inspirational Network (INSP).

McBath earned a bachelor's and master's degree respectively from the Massachusetts Institute of Technology (MIT) and Regent University. He also holds a doctor of ministry degree from Providence Bible College and Theological Seminary, where he is a visiting professor and member of the board of directors. Additionally, McBath serves on the board of advisors for *Ministries Today* magazine, among other organizations.

He lives in Chesapeake, Virginia, with his wife and copastor, Janeen, and their five children.

To contact the author:

Revival Word Ministries
5847 Poplar Hall Drive
Suite 204
Norfolk, VA 23502
www.revivalword.org